The Guide to a **Smart** Divorce

Experts' advice for surviving divorce

by
The Divorce Team

Kristine Turner, Ph.D.
David W. Heckenbach, Esq.
Kim Langelaar, CDFA™
Kurt Groesser, Realtor ®, MBA
Jan Parsons, Senior Mortgage Banker

A Books To Believe In Publication

Copyright © 2011 - The Divorce Team:
Kristine Turner, Ph.D. & David W. Heckenbach, Esq. & Kim Langelaar, CDFA™& Kurt Groesser & Jan Parsons

Castle Rock, CO 80203

Proudly Published in the USA by
Thornton Publishing, Inc.
17011 Lincoln Ave. #408
Parker, CO 80134

Phone: 303.794.8888
Fax: 720.863.2013

Edited by
Dianne Lorang, The Write Help, LLC
Phone: 303.738.0102
www.TheWriteHelp.wordpress.com
DianneL@msn.com

www.DivorceAdvice360.com

ISBN: 0-9846342-0-7

DEDICATION

We dedicate this guide to those of you going through divorce. Although divorce can be difficult, it doesn't have to be devastating. Many families grow and thrive during the divorce process. With the right information, you can manage your divorce successfully, grow from the experience, and achieve positive results.

May this information serve you and your family well.

TABLE OF CONTENTS

Throughout the book, you'll see these boxes and these are little stories from us or from clients we've served.

These stories are the "I wish I'd have known..." real-life, 'learned the hard way' lessons that we hope we can spare all of you.

FOREWORD

Divorce is difficult, but it doesn't have to be devastating.

After having spent years working in the field of divorce, we of The Divorce Team collaborated to create this comprehensive yet easy-to-read guide for people going through divorce. If you are like most people, you did not plan to divorce and therefore are not prepared for the challenge. Divorce is a journey, and there are better and worse paths to take while moving through it. This guide is intended to help you think through the myriad of issues that arise and maneuver through your divorce effectively.

We are sure you have a number of questions about how to work through your divorce issues. Perhaps you need help with your parenting plan or you would like guidance on selling your house. Perhaps you need legal assistance or financial consultation. This guide was written in an easy-to-use format so that you can quickly get the information you need. You can also peruse other sections of this guide to help stimulate thinking around topics you may not have considered prior to filing for divorce.

This book was written with you in mind. We hope you find it helpful, and we wish you the best of luck getting through this transition in your life.

"The best thing I did for myself during the divorce process was to 'appreciate myself.' I actually thanked myself for working hard to have a positive divorce situation for my kids' sake and, in the end, it was for my sake, too."

INTRODUCTION:
YOUR OPTIONS

Divorce is a major decision and a huge transition in life. Although it will undoubtedly be a lot of work to finalize your divorce settlement, the basic objective is to divide your assets and/or debt. If you have children, you will also need to provide a parenting plan for the courts to review. This divorce guide is designed to give you an overview of the divorce process, a few "tricks of the trade" and clarification on a variety of issues to help you determine the best course of action to finalize your divorce fairly and reasonably.

When you tell your family and friends that you have decided to get a divorce, they will do one or two of several things: say they are sorry, ask you why, try to talk you out of it, and give you unsolicited advice. They mean well, but at this point, you have already been through the heart-wrenching decision to get a divorce and are probably fairly confident you are doing the right thing. So although it is beneficial to have family and friends as part of your support system, they are not the best ones to approach for legal, financial, or even emotional advice.

What you need are professionals who know all the ins and outs of the divorce process, who have "been there, done that!" We of The Divorce Team are all experienced both professionally and personally in some or many aspects of divorce. In collaborating with one another on this book, we have learned that if we don't know something, we certainly know someone who does know or who can find out. Your family and friends, even if they know a few things about divorce, are too close to you to be objective. What you need are professionals who understand that your divorce outcome will depend on a lot of variables, such as the divorce law where you live, current parenting trends, and what option you use to make your divorce legal.

You may think that there is only one means to this end, hiring an expensive attorney. But there is a continuum of options available for people going through divorce. Filing Pro Se is at one end of that continuum, while hiring an attorney to go to court for you is at the other end. The cost and the amount of time it will take to reach a settlement or agreement in your divorce will follow that same continuum. Typically, the more people you bring into your case, the longer it will take and the more it will cost. Before you spend a lot of time, energy, and money on your divorce, it's important to know what you are paying for and what you will likely get for your money.

PRO SE

About half the people going through divorce decide to file Pro Se. They file all of their own paperwork with the courts and they do it without any help from an attorney. If you file Pro Se you will be doing all of the work yourself. You can find all of the paperwork on court websites, and most courts have a Pro Se center where you can ask some questions about how to file everything properly. Some courts host classes or lunches where attorneys come and help you fill out your paperwork for free. If you can reach an agreement (settlement) on your own, it will be the least expensive, and it will set a precedence that demonstrates your ability to resolve your differences when they arise in the future. For example, if you have children, you are likely to have many discussions and decisions to make moving forward post decree (after your divorce is final).

MEDIATION

For the issues you can't resolve on your own, many courts will now mandate that you seek mediation before coming to court. You can choose to hire a mediator or the courts can appoint one for you.

A mediator acts as a neutral third party. They usually have a legal or mental health background and have been trained in mediation techniques. To resolve your differences, the mediator will work with you and your "spouse" either in the same office or separate rooms depending upon the level of conflict in your case. A mediator can work alone or you can bring your attorney(s) to mediation.

Your mediator will not decide your case for you; the decision-making power remains with you and your "spouse." Instead, a mediator will guide you in making reasonable decisions, for example, about the division of your assets and parenting plans (if you have children).

A mediator may help educate you about the process of divorce as well as remind you about all the details you will need to take care of or consider in your settlement, such as getting an appraisal on your house or splitting vacation time with the children. The beauty of mediation is that these decisions remain under your control. You don't turn them over to a third party.

ARBITRATION

If you opt for arbitration, it will play out like mediation but you will have given the arbitrator the decision-making power if you can't reach an agreement. In other words, if you can't finalize a settlement after meeting with the arbitrator for a couple of sessions, that person will put on a different hat, so to speak, and make the decision for you. Their decision becomes binding and gets filed with the court whether you like the decision or not.

RENT A JUDGE

Some couples find that they still want a judge to settle their differences, but they don't want to wait for the courts to hear their case. One option is to "rent a judge." Usually, your attorneys will represent you in a full blown hearing, but it will likely occur in a conference room versus a court room. You will also be paying the judge to attend the hearing, hence the term "rent a judge." As with arbitrator, the judge will make the decision for you and file it with the court.

CHILD AND FAMILY INVESTIGATOR*

If you are having trouble deciding upon a parenting plan for your children, you may want to hire a CFI (child and family investigator) to help you. This is usually a mental health professional who is also trained as a CFI.

This neutral third party will spend upwards of 40 hours meeting with your family, meeting with your children, and talking to your friends, neighbors, the grandparents, and/or children's teachers in order to make a determination as to the best parenting plan for your children. Note that the CFI will determine what is best for the children, not what is best for the parents.

A CFI can be very helpful in determining a parenting plan, but the process can be very difficult. For example, a CFI's report usually includes a personality assessment of both parents which can feel quite intrusive. You may struggle to present yourself in a positive manner during your evaluation when you are at your worst, not at your best. Then at a time that has probably made you feel vulnerable, it can be difficult to read the CFI's report section that indicates your strengths and weaknesses as a parent.

Although the CFI's report is only a recommendation on what you should do in regard to your parenting plan, it holds a lot of weight once it gets turned over to a judge or other decision maker. By hiring a CFI, you have turned some of the decision-making power over to a third party.

---

*This is the Colorado term. In other states, it may be called Custody or Parenting Time Evaluator or another name.

Parenting Coordinator and Decision Maker

The PC/DM (parenting coordinator and decision maker) is another avenue to help you resolve disputes. These individuals are usually brought into a case post decree or after you have a settlement in place. Many people make the mistake of thinking that the divorce will end when they reach a settlement, file their paperwork with the court, and get their dissolution of marriage. However, you will likely find that you have to continue to interact with your former spouse if you have children. You will often need to make changes to your parenting plan throughout the years. This can be accomplished in all the previous methods above or through a PC/DM.

A PC/DM is usually a mental health or legal professional trained in PC/DM work. You will typically assign someone to your case; when an issue arises that you can't resolve, you will meet with your PC/DM to help you determine an agreement. Some PC/DM's will act more like mediators; others will have been given decision-making authority.

A typical case might go something like this: a couple has a parenting plan in place that says they each get two weeks of vacation with their children every summer. This works fine for the first two years, but in the third year, there's an overlap in their requests for vacation time. Mom wants to take the children to her sister's wedding in Hawaii at the same time Dad wants to take the kids to his family reunion in Maine.

If the parenting plan does not designate who gets priority vacation in odd or even years, the couple may come to an impasse. In this situation, they would call on their PC/DM to help them determine an agreement. If they cannot come to an agreement, the PC/DM will decide for them and enter the decision as a court order. In other words, the parents will lose their decision-making power if they can't make a decision together.

COLLABORATIVE LAW

Collaborative law is slightly different from hiring conventional family attorneys. In collaborative law, you and your "spouse" will agree ahead of time to hire collaborative law attorneys who will adhere to a specific collaborative process in reaching a settlement. You and your attorneys will attend negotiation meetings in conference rooms, the intent being to reach a settlement without going to court (litigation). However, if you can't reach a settlement and need to go to court, your collaborative law attorneys will resign from your case and you will need to start all over again with new legal counsel.

LITIGATION

Only about five percent of divorce cases actually go through litigation. Many more go through the process of preparing for it only to settle at the last minute to avoid the stress of litigation. It's not unusual for a case to resolve itself in the hallway of the court building right before it is to be heard by the judge.

To prepare for litigation, you and your "spouse" will hire your own attorneys who will take you through the process of discovery, which is sharing of all pertinent information related to finances and parenting. Then every effort is usually made to reach a settlement through avenues mentioned above, such as mediation and arbitration. The decisions that cannot be reached through negotiation are left to the courts.

Those include dividing property and debt, determining child and/or spousal support and sanctioning parenting plans. Your particular resolutions will depend on a combination of the laws of the state as well as the judges involved.

Bottom line: Not only does litigation leave important life decisions to the courts, but it is the most expensive and time-consuming means to an end, often taking up to a year to complete.

Whichever means you choose to legally dissolve your marriage and make decisions before and after your divorce, it is important to know all of your options. It is also important to let your family and friends know that this is your decision, just as getting a divorce is your decision. The more you are in charge, the better you will feel about the whole process, and the easier it will be.

Remember, divorce is difficult but it doesn't have to be devastating.

LEGAL
ADVICE

DAVID W. HECKENBACH, ESQ.

Dave's Personal Story

I knew my divorce was coming. I knew it for months. I had been physically separated from my wife and had been "emotionally divorced" for some time. Yet when my wife filed for divorce, she exhibited a range of emotions indicating she was not at the same point. I felt helpless and worried about my relationship with our children. We went from contested court hearings at every stage and through multiple custody evaluations.

With the passage of time, however, we were able to put explosive acrimony aside for the sake of our children and also to preserve the quality of our own lives. It is with great gratitude I can say that I have enjoyed a healthy working relationship with my ex-wife for many years now. Never did our children flourish more than from the day their mother and I moved forward, forgave and placed their needs ahead of our own.

Today I tell my clients, "No matter how tough you think you are, no matter how emotionally prepared you believe you are, I can guarantee that you will not have anticipated all the negative emotions, the fears, the uncertainty, and the sense of loss and failure the divorce process generates." I am also able to tell them that they will be okay, there will be healing, there will be happiness and there can be a higher quality of life after divorce.

SO MANY LAWYERS, SO LITTLE TIME

The divorce process can be simple and direct but many times it is not. When disputes regarding your children and their future arise, you want a competent lawyer at your side. When you consider that a divorce can be the single largest financial transaction of your adult life, you need an expert attorney to help you strategize. You will want to hire the best lawyer possible to achieve your goals over the course of the divorce process.

Almost everyone knows a divorce lawyer or someone who has gone through a divorce. There are many lawyers who claim to be qualified to handle even the most complex divorces. However, in my opinion, the number of truly competent family law practitioners makes up a small pool from which to draw. These attorneys place their clients' needs ahead of their own while having the experience, intelligence, and reputation that set them apart from the crowd.

REPUTATION IS GOLDEN

In your search for a good lawyer to help you through your divorce process, there are several precepts that should play into your decision. Most important, your lawyer needs to be respected in their community. No matter how much experience a lawyer has or claims to have, if they do not enjoy a good reputation for truth and veracity, competency and preparedness, they will not be well-received by the ultimate audience, the judge.

It is always preferable to settle a case rather than let the judge decide the fate of your children's future as well as your financial future. But in a small percentage of cases, judges must make the decisions. So although you should go into the process hoping for an expeditious and reasonable resolution, you should prepare for litigation before a judicial officer. If that judge does not know, does not respect or dislikes your attorney, you are disadvantaged.

Therefore, when you interview attorneys (and you should interview several), ask about their specific experiences in the jurisdiction in which your case will be filed, including their relationship with the judges and other judicial officers. An attorney can be imminently qualified with decades of experience, but if they are not known in your jurisdiction, it is a distinct possibility that the "good old boy" or "good old girl" on the other side will enjoy more positive results.

Bottom line: Make sure that your selection of an attorney is one who has specific experience and a solid reputation in your jurisdiction and with the judges who handle family law matters.

Word of Mouth

An obvious resource to narrow your choice of attorneys is through those who have "been there, done that!" Don't just ask about their own divorce attorneys but about the attorneys on the other side. I am surprised by how many referrals I get from opposing parties who felt I did a good job and perhaps "out-lawyered" their own attorneys. And don't take the word of just one friend or family member. Just as you should interview several attorneys, you should talk to a variety of friends and associates.

PUBLISHED RESOURCE MATERIALS

There are a variety of published rating systems and distinctions that can be afforded practitioners. Probably the most notable resource is that of *Martindale-Hubbell* ® (www.Martindale.com), largely recognized for its peer-rating system. In order to achieve any sort of rating, an attorney must have been in practice for a certain number of years and meet minimum evaluative ethical criteria.

There are three general classes of ratings within *Martindale-Hubbell* ®. A-V is the highest, B-V is the next highest, followed by C-V. The "V" stands for "very" high ethical standards and the A, B, C standards are similar to grades you received in school. Attorneys who have achieved an A-V rating from *Martindale-Hubbell* ® are viewed by other lawyers and judges as highly ethical and very talented. That is not to say that you cannot find a good lawyer with either a B-V or even a C-V rating. It simply means that their peers familiar with their work believe them to be better or less so than other lawyers.

There is also an elite group of attorneys who first meet the criteria for an A-V rating and then are afforded the status of "Preeminent Lawyers." If you choose an attorney with an A-V Preeminent rating, you most likely have will have an attorney of extraordinary intellect, talent and skill.

While *Martindale-Hubbell* ® is probably the best known published resource, there are many others to help you in your selection of an attorney. An important one is membership in the local and/or national affiliate of the Academy of Matrimonial Attorneys (www.AAML.org). Although requirements for admission into these clubs vary from state to state, membership is generally restricted to those who limit their practices to family law.

One of the emerging arenas for attorney recognition is the "Super Lawyers" classification system, which, like *Martindale-Hubbell* ®, involves a listing of peer-rated attorneys who are in the top 5% of the lawyers practicing in their state. You can find this rating system at www.SuperLawyers.com.

There are any number of other groups, clubs and entities that either are or purport to be resource guides for the selection of an attorney but are too numerous to mention here. Regardless, your selection process circles back to finding a lawyer who is well respected, is smart, is a good strategist, and has significant experience with your type of case and in your specific jurisdiction.

A word of caution is in order. Exercise care and discernment when a lawyer holds themselves out as one with particular specializations. For example, there are a great number of lawyers that are qualified to assist fathers in exercising their rights; but if a lawyer is advertising as a "Father's Rights" specialist, they may be using that tag line as a hook just to get clients because they do not receive referrals from other lawyers. You should always seek out the best-qualified lawyer, not just someone that advertises specialties.

HOURLY RATES

Hourly rates can fluctuate wildly, but generally speaking the more experienced lawyers, the busier lawyers and the lawyers that enjoy better reputations with the judges are going to cost more. That is not to say that you cannot find a very bright "up and comer" that does not charge an arm-and-a-leg. After all, the "old dogs" that are charging significant hourly rates were once in that category at some point in their careers.

One of the most common questions I get during initial consultation is "How much will this cost?" After 31 years of practice, many as a family law practitioner, I have yet to come up with a good answer to this question. There are far too many variables. Even if you were the most reasonable, manageable, empathetic client, it is impossible to control the behavior of the other side.

Of the four people typically involved in a divorce, the two parties and their respective attorneys, it only takes one to make the process thorny, protracted and expensive for all concerned. The amount your case will cost is directly proportionate to the amount of disagreement there arises between you and your "spouse." Because emotions are almost always raw, there are usually more problems than initially anticipated.

Another factor to consider is efficiency. An attorney who charges $500 per hour may very well be able to accomplish in three hours what takes the $250-per-hour attorney ten hours to do. There are always tradeoffs.

In my firm as in most, we assign a task to the person with the lowest hourly rate capable of a particular service. For example, organization of discovery documents is performed by a paralegal; research and motion drafting is done by a mid-level or even beginning associate; and trial strategies and the trial itself are conducted by a senior attorney. This is not the case should you choose a solo practitioner who in the end may cost you more because they charge every detail at their hourly rate.

Therefore, it is not necessarily wise to make your choice of attorney based on hourly rates alone. If an attorney enjoys a good reputation and is part of a reliable firm, although expensive, they may end up costing you less than a cheaper attorney with a bad or no reputation who is working on their own.

PERSONALITIES

As with any group of professionals, lawyers have different personalities. Some are more empathetic than others; some are better communicators than others; and some are more cut-throat than others. The critical component with picking a personality is that you as the client have a high level of comfort as well as confidence in who you have selected. Divorce is often a terribly emotional experience. The fear of the unknown with respect to your children and your financial future can be overwhelming.

Therefore, you should always interview several lawyers that meet your criteria in terms of experience and reputation to ensure your comfort level with the one you ultimately choose. On paper, you might have three lawyers with virtually identical qualifications, years of experience and reputation, yet you may find they have three distinct personalities.

Hopefully, you will feel comfortable with at least one of the attorneys you have chosen to interview. But if you don't, you can widen your search until you find the perfect fit for you. You don't want to be switching lawyers in midstream. When a judge sees a client who has changed attorneys two or more times during their divorce, they understandably come to believe that the client is the one who is unreasonable rather than the other side. That is not to say that your initial decision may not be the right one for you. But without a substantial reason for changing counsel, it is rarely a good idea to do so.

Therefore, it is important to make the best choice possible according to recommendations, ratings, reputations, and your own gut instinct. In the end, go with the most qualified attorney with whom you feel the highest level of comfort and personal rapport. Divorce is too difficult a process to go through with someone you dislike. While you may not become best friends with your attorney, it is necessary to have a collaborative and respectful relationship.

WORKING WITH
YOUR ATTORNEY

If you have decided to be represented in your divorce by an attorney, there will be a cost, no doubt. But the amount of that cost is in part attributable to your conduct and behavior throughout the course of the process. As noted previously, the more disagreement, the more expense. And while it only takes one person involved to run costs up for everyone, there are ways to contain the amount of your attorney's bill.

Further, there are ways to contain and define the range of risks with which you engage during the divorce process. A saying I share with most of my clients is that two experienced attorneys with two reasonable clients can carve up a marital estate with a scalpel in a way that healing can begin quickly. In contrast, allowing a judge to decide your case is similar to sitting in the front row of the comedian Gallagher's show where he takes a sledge hammer and smashes the watermelon (your marital estate) and whatever sticks to you, you keep, whatever sticks to your "spouse," they keep.

Clearly, it is not always possible to settle cases. Sometimes there are disputes with regard to the welfare of children that have the parties so polarized the judge must make the decision. When there are substantial disagreements regarding the marital character of assets or the amount of spousal support, litigation may be the only way to resolve the case. But if at all possible, both parties should make every reasonable attempt to settle the case out of court. To that end, you can only control your side of things. By acting in good faith, you will do all you can to help minimize your cost.

COOPERATING WITH
YOUR ATTORNEY

Divorce entails sharing a great deal of information with each side. You and your "spouse" will be required to exchange all pertinent financial information and all materials regarding minor children. There are basically two ways to proceed with this process. The first is to make every effort to assemble your documents in an organized fashion for your attorney. Otherwise you will have to pay for your attorney's staff to hunt for, sort through and identify pertinent documents.

The second and less intelligent way is to play games by attempting to hide money/assets or delaying your response to requests for obligatory and mandated disclosures and discovery. If you do not comply, you will end up paying your attorney or the other side's for their time spent playing your game. One way or the other, the necessary information will be obtained because it is your attorney's ethical charge to produce it. The higher your level of cooperation with this endeavor, the less expensive it will be for you.

USING DISCRETION IN CONTACTING YOUR ATTORNEY

Using discretion in contacting your attorney can be difficult. Emotions are running at their peak and even the slightest perceived infraction by the other side can spark tremendous anger and frustration. Calling or emailing your attorney each time your spouse has the children back seven minutes late will cost just as much as calling or sending an email about the $500,000 disparity between your expert's business evaluation and the other side's.

While you should never hesitate to contact your attorney about matters of importance, you need to let a little bit of time pass before reacting and contacting your attorney over issues that will not make a material difference in your case. If anything, keep a journal or a log, but do not waste your money and your attorney's time on minor issues that will not affect the outcome of your divorce.

REASONABLENESS

It is important to recognize and accept that this is going to be a highly charged emotional time for you and your "spouse." There are feelings of betrayal, anger, mistrust and frustration in nearly every divorce proceeding. Pride, "the principle of the thing" and "money to spend" are your lawyer's meal tickets and they will lead to issues and asset depletion that you will regret in the not-so-distant future.

And while recognizing that the other side may be petty, malicious or vindictive, you have little chance of changing their behavior. You probably couldn't control their behavior during the marriage, so you certainly can't now. All you can do is control your side of things.

That is not to say that it is inappropriate to react in a legal and measured way when your spouse violates court orders or fails to properly disclose assets that are to be divided. Rather, it is up to you to make every effort to behave reasonably, to listen to the advice of the attorney you have chosen. The more reasonable, candid, and cooperative you are, the more effective your lawyer can be and the less expensive your divorce will be.

While it is unwritten, most divorce practitioners recognize what we have affectionately come to call the "Son-of-a-Bitch Rule." Attorneys and clients that underestimate this rule find themselves walking out the courtroom with their tail between their legs, feeling hammered by the presiding judicial officer.

This rule is simple: judges are human beings. Even in a "no fault" state, if they perceive that one of the parties has behaved badly during the course of the divorce, if that person has been deceitful, tried to hide assets, or in any way been unreasonable, the judge may make them pay dearly.

Plus judges in domestic cases have wide latitude; it is extremely difficult to get such cases reversed on appeal because the legal standard is whether or not there is evidence in the record to support the judge's findings or if the judge abused their discretion in entering the orders. The appellate court will not substitute its personal judgment for that of a trial judge.

No matter what, if you have to litigate your case you do not want to be perceived as the "Son of a Bitch" that will one way or the other be punished by the judge. Therefore, if your attorney tells you that the judge won't appreciate what you are trying to do, listen. As a litigator, nothing suits me more than walking into a courtroom with a client who has been reasonable when the other side has not played by the rules.

Playing games results in loosing discretionary calls to the other side at the hands of the judge as well as increased costs, perhaps even being sanctioned to pay the other side's attorney fees. Behaving reasonably, cooperatively and decently keeps your costs down and maximizes your position in front of the judge.

> *"I kept wanting to make my former spouse pay for the hurt and pain she had caused me, and I wanted to minimize her child support and maintenance in order to do this. It wasn't until three years post divorce and a number of nasty trips to court that I realized that no matter how much I did or didn't have to pay her, it would never heal the wounds inside of me. I had to heal these emotional injuries in a healthy way. I had to overcome my own hurt and pain irrespective of how she chose to live her life."*

FINANCIAL ADVICE

KIM LANGELAAR, CDFA™

Kim's Personal Story

Stepping back fifteen years ago when I first started my divorce process, I was a young stay-at-home mom. I had two toddlers and zero family members in the state. I had trusted my husband with my life. I felt like I was at risk of becoming a bag lady. Like many women, I had made the mistake of giving control of the family finances to my husband while I raised the children.

Fortunately, I had been on my own before marriage and had managed my own finances. Nevertheless, I was not prepared for the complexity of splitting marital assets. I did not even know what a marital asset was before the divorce. On the other hand, my "spouse" was surrounded by working adults and had many more resources to find the advice he needed on dividing said assets.

Even after the divorce, because my ex-husband was reluctant to cooperate with the court order division of retirement assets, I had difficulty actually getting the assets that had been awarded to me. Six months later, $7000 more in attorney fees, when I finally received the stock I had been awarded, it was only worth $10 a share when it had been worth $100 a share at the time of the divorce. With proper planning, this could have been avoided.

Because of my own experience and that of others who have shared similar stories with me, I decided to write the Financial Advice chapter of this book. It provides basic terminology and information only about the divorce financial process and is not intended to substitute for the advice of a financial professional, such as myself or your attorney. I wish you the best of luck.

FINANCIAL ASPECTS OF DIVORCE

Probably the most difficult issue when a couple divorces besides their parenting plan is finances. There are more money issues to be addressed than you may realize. The earlier you start planning financially for your divorce, the better you will be in the long run. You will need time to prepare for and then adjust to your new financial life. This chapter speaks to the many things you can consider and do before, during and after filing for divorce that will help improve your financial future.

DOCUMENT GATHERING

If you are the spouse asking for the divorce, you have had some time to think about the financial ramifications. You may have done a little preparing before you approached you partner about a divorce. In which case, you are at an advantage. If you are the not-so-prepared spouse you will have some catching up to do, especially if you have not been handling the finances. You need to understand that your "spouse" will have been thinking (maybe even plotting) about what they want. Now is the time for you to take a crash course on every aspect of your family's finances.

There are many documents you need to find and make copies of as soon as you know there is a divorce in your future. If in doubt about a document, make a copy of it. Once you have gathered all your financial information, you and your professional can assess your financial picture and determine debt to income ratio.

DOCUMENTS YOU WILL NEED

❖ All credit card statements

❖ All retirement accounts

❖ All investment accounts

❖ Any loans and their account numbers

❖ Tax returns for the last three years (five years if you own a business)

❖ Pay stubs, W-2's and 1099 forms

❖ Employee benefit packages

❖ Airline frequent flier miles

❖ Wills and Trusts

❖ Any legal document that pertains to money

❖ Credit reports

DEBT

It makes financial sense to start off your new life with the least amount of debt as possible. Start by trying to work with your "spouse" to pay off as much debt as you can before you start the divorce process. The cleaner your financial situation, the easier it will be to split the marital assets and debt. Consider that you can spend much time, effort and money in an attorney's office figuring out how to pay off debt, or you can proactively work together to do so before it gets to that point. If this is not feasible with your "spouse," seek out a financial professional to advise you on your options regarding your debt.

BUDGETING

This may be the first time you have had to actually look at the family finances. In many marriages, one partner takes care of all the bills and filing taxes. If you haven't taken part previous to your divorce, or even if you have, now is the time to educate yourself on your living expenses versus your lifestyle expenses:

Living Expenses: **Necessary expenses to live on**

Lifestyle Expenses: **Unnecessary expenses we live by**

Everyone knows they need shelter, transportation, clothing and food. But do we need a 6000-squre-foot house, a Porsche, designer-label clothing and filet mignon and lobster for dinner once a week? I know this sounds extreme, but the truth is that many two-income families in today's credit-card society mistakenly think that Starbucks, for example, is a necessary expense rather than a lifestyle choice.

The reality for most divorcing couples will be the need to change their lifestyles, at least for a few years. This does not mean you can't have a treat now and then; you will just need to budget for it. Divorce is a great opportunity to evaluate what you want your life to look like and then design it to fit you budget.

EXPENSES

During separation, finances can get tough for a lot of couples. If you have never had to budget, this is the time to learn how. Believe it or not, you can make it fun. You'll find that there are free days at zoos and museums, for example, which take some planning but are well worth the time and effort. You can challenge yourself to find ways to save on groceries, such as buying in bulk and using coupons which can save you hundreds of dollars per year.

While food is a necessary expense, other items that can be cut are lifestyle choices such as cable or satellite TV. Do you really need 300 channels or would basic TV be enough? When I first divorced, I decided to ditch the cable and rent movies. Five years later, I subscribed to all the premium channels and on-demand movies. I found I missed the times we spent as a family going to the store to pick out a movie that we would watch together.

I learned that less does not necessarily mean a lower quality of life. It just means simplifying. I know of one father who did not have the money or the energy for the annual camping trip he used to take with his children. Instead, he set up the tent in the backyard, made popcorn and told stories to his children. They loved it!

Another tip: if you and your "spouse" are on good enough terms, discuss how to share items between the two households. These may include, if you live close enough, the lawn mower, power tools and the children's bikes and skateboards. In time, you may be able to purchase your own, but at first sharing will help with the financial shock of two households versus one.

❖　❖　❖

TIP

Cutting expenses will help you to adjust to the lower family income that will most likely occur. However, finding ways for your money to work for you is your ultimate goal, for example, investing in your education, the stock market or real estate, or building a business. A financial professional can help you decide which options are best for your situation.

WAYS TO CUT SPENDING

❖   Downsize your home, vehicle or both

❖   Shop around for home and car insurance

❖   Cut cable or satellite TV (rent movies instead)

❖   Go to the public library for books, magazines, and DVDs (TV shows as well as popular movies)

❖   Use coupons (sign up for www.Groupon.com and check out www.Entertainment.com)

❖   Eat at home and pack lunches (often healthier)

❖   Bulk shop, but only if you will use the items (sometimes sales afford better savings)

❖   Comparison shop items before buying (waiting will sometimes make an item unnecessary)

❖   Cut club memberships (bargains can be found)

❖   Limit your children's paid activities (they will have more time for homework, fun and family)

SHOW ME THE MONEY!

For most of my clients, the number one issue is maintaining positive cash flow, not only the ability to pay the bills on a monthly basis after the divorce, but five, ten and fifteen years down the road. To meet cash flow needs, there are three sources of money that may be available to you: child support, spousal support, and marital property and assets.

Young stay-at-home moms often ask me the following: "Do I have to go back to work before my children start school?" A mother's lifestyle staying home with her children versus earning income will be quite different. A client and I will come up with a budget based on what they want their life to look like. We will examine their living expenses and come up with a realistic lifestyle analysis, which they will then take to their attorney who will advise them on what various settlements will afford them.

I am a firm believer that you can design the life you want with realistic boundaries and planning. For many young mothers, staying home with their children is very important to them; however, there is an "opportunity cost" involved. For example, they may need to take vacations in state or visiting relatives rather than flying to a tropical island like they did while married. The point is that knowledge is your power and with it you will make the best decisions for you and your family.

CHILD SUPPORT

Child support is non-taxable income to the person receiving it and not tax-deductible by the person paying it. (A tax professional will help you determine which parent gets to use the dependent deduction on their taxes.) Plus the child support formula does NOT take into consideration all the child's actual expenses, for example, extra-curricular activities, private-school tuition and college funding. You and your "spouse" will need to decide on how to pay for these expenses or alter your lifestyle and expectations.

SPOUSAL SUPPORT

It may be applicable for you or your "spouse" to have spousal support for a few years after the marriage. Spousal support is usually based on need and the ability to pay. A judge will look at different factors according to your state law to determine if spousal support is appropriate.

Spousal support is typically taxable to the person receiving it and tax-deductible to the person paying it. However, there are tax laws specific to divorce so you would be wise to consult with a professional to help you plan your financial future.

If you are to receive spousal support for a few years, this money is expected to help you reestablish yourself financially, to become independent. A judge rarely awards lifetime support. It might seem like you will have plenty of time, but the day spousal support ends will come sooner than later. You need to use this money and time wisely to prepare yourself for the future when you will need to earn an income according to your lifestyle choices.

MARITAL PROPERTY AND ASSETS

What state you are getting your divorce in will determine if the judge sees marital property division as an equal split or an equitable split. In other words, even if the marital property is split equally, it may not be equal. Let's say the equity in your house is $300,000 and you have an investment account worth $300,000. This does not mean the after-tax value will be equal. A lot will depend on the market and costs when you sell your house compared to the growth or losses in the investment account when sold.

Also, getting the marital home comes with the cost and time to maintain it when this was probably shared by both parties before the divorce. You need to take everything into consideration before thinking you're getting the best deal. The point is that marital property and assets of equal equity are not of equal value.

❖　❖　❖

TIP
Property that is separate can possibly become marital if not kept separately.

MANAGING
RISK

Divorce is a time to evaluate your insurance policies. Some couples feel comfortable staying with the same insurance or financial professional they worked with while married. However, it has been my experience that one of the parties usually has a closer relationship with the professional. That tends to leave the other party feeling uncomfortable working with the same person. If you find yourself in this position, I recommend searching for another professional to help you with your insurance or financial needs.

LIFE INSURANCE:

You will definitely want to review the life insurance policies before your divorce is final. It is common practice for the divorce decree to require spousal support and/or child support be secured by a life insurance policy. If you are the spouse receiving the proceeds from said policy, I recommend that you are also the owner of the policy. This way if the policy is cancelled for any reason, such as for non-payment or if your "spouse" has changed beneficiaries, you get the notice.

Because it is common for attorneys to order each party to show proof of a life insurance policy once a year, you may ask why it is important that you are the owner of the policy. One reason is save yourself attorney fees; a second more important reason is that

THE GUIDE TO A SMART DIVORCE

your "spouse" may die during the year and may have not kept the life insurance policy current.

If you decide to keep your ex-spouse as the beneficiary, make sure you get written notice from the life insurance company acknowledging that the beneficiary is your ex-spouse. I had a client who told me that when her ex-husband died, he did want her to stay beneficiary of the existing life insurance policy. He even reassured her two days before his death not to worry, she was the beneficiary of his policy. Unfortunately, he died and although he was true to his word, she was listed as beneficiary, the language in the policy listed her as spouse and not ex-spouse. Because of the law in her state, she did not receive the life insurance benefit.

The children were listed second as beneficiaries, but their mother had to go through probate to receive the money for them. It was a very complicated and expensive experience for all of them. In this case, the language in the divorce decree was not enough to enforce her ex-husband's wishes. (To make matters worse, he did not have a will or trust in place, which was poor planning on his part.)

DISABILITY INSURANCE:

If you are required to pay or are receiving spousal or child support, disability insurance is another vehicle that can replace income should the need arise. It is designed should a person become ill or sustain an injury preventing them from earning an income in their occupation. Disability insurance is not one-size-fits-all; the premium depends on the insured's occupation and income as well as if they own a business. It is advisable to shop through an insurance professional.

HEALTH INSURANCE:

If you are/were covered on your "spouse's" group health insurance, you will have the option of being placed on COBRA (Consolidated Omnibus Budget Reconciliation Act) for 36 months. As the law stands, after 36 months you will either need to find an individual health plan or be employed with a company that offers group health insurance. If you have a pre-existing condition or develop a sickness during the time you are on COBRA, it may be more difficult or impossible to get individual healthcare coverage in some states until the new healthcare reform law goes into effect in 2014. (Check with your local health insurance agent.)

❖   ❖   ❖

TIP
There are deadlines for enrolling for COBRA that need to be met or you will lose your opportunity to be placed on COBRA.

Auto/Home Insurance:

Once you are divorced, you will need to have your own auto and home insurance policies. If you are renting during the divorce and have taken items of value with you, you may want to purchase renters insurance.

If you have a teenage driver, talk with your insurance agent about coverage. Depending on whose vehicle the teen is driving and how many times they have access to your vehicle may determine if you or your "spouse" need to purchase coverage.

❖ ❖ ❖

TIP

Independent insurance agents are a good choice as they represent multiple companies and spend time shopping insurance companies for you. The only downside is the time it takes for them to find a competitive product for you. Your patience, however, will usually pay out.

Taxes

Spousal Support:

As indicated previously, spousal support is typically treated as taxable income to the person receiving it and tax-deductible for the person paying it. Therefore, it's important to determine what your net income or out-of-pocket cost will be.

Let's just say you have been the stay-at-home spouse for years. Is it better to receive a smaller amount of spousal support for several years rather than a larger amount for a few years? Perhaps your plan is to go back to school. Did you know the amount of spousal support received may impact the amount of financial aid you may be entitled to receive, not to mention your tax liability? A financial professional helping you analyze this will help your attorney negotiate your settlement.

BUSINESS EVALUATIONS:

Taxes can get very complicated if you and/or your "spouse" own a business. Some items that are deductible as a business owner may not be deductible once you're divorced. It is advisable for you to work with a professional knowledgeable with both business taxes and divorce.

RETIREMENT

DEFINED CONTRIBUTION PLAN:

A defined contribution plan retirement account has an actual cash value today. A 401K is one type. These usually can't be accessed before you reach age 59½ without incurring a 10% penalty for early withdrawal.

When you get divorced, you are allowed to withdraw your portion from your "spouse's" accounts before retirement without triggering the penalty. However, if you do not roll the money directly into another retirement account within a period of time, you will have to pay taxes on the portion you withdrew.

DEFINED BENEFIT PLAN/PENSION:

A defined benefit plan/pension is the monthly income a company promises to pay a retiree for the rest of their life. Generally speaking, you can't access the money until you retire, although some plans allow for a lump-sum transfer at the time of a divorce.

DIVIDING RETIREMENT PLANS:

Not all retirement plans are created equal. Retirement plans can have benefits such as cost-of-living expenses, survivor benefits and other benefits you may not be aware of. Most company plans are divided by a QDRO (Qualified Domestic Relation Order). A QDRO is not dictated by the courts but by the plan administrator. You should ask the administrator if they can provide you with standard forms for division of your plan.

I would suggest working with a QDRO expert to advise you on how to write this part of your separation agreement. A good reason to use someone familiar with both law and accounting is that the wording of your divorce decree should coincide with the wording of your QDRO.

SOCIAL SECURITY BENEFITS:

If you have been married for ten years or more, you will be entitled to one-half of your "spouse's" Social Security benefit or 100% of your own benefit, whichever is greater. This does not impact your "spouse's" Social Security benefit in any way.

ONCE YOUR DIVORCE IS FINAL

Once you are divorced, you may be tempted to try out marriage again. If you had assets awarded to you from your first marriage, protect them for the benefit of you and your children. Statistically, second marriages have a greater chance of failing than first marriages. Be smart and keep your assets separate; don't spend them frivolously on a second spouse.

Set expectations with your new spouse before you get married. It would be wise to see a financial planner to talk about how you will conduct your financial life together. There is nothing worse to find out your values and goals concerning "his, her and our money" are dramatically different than each other's once married.

❖ ❖ ❖

TIP
Remarriage is a financial affair. Protect your retirement and your children.

There is much to consider financially when planning your divorce. It will take detailed information, preparation, planning, and a lot of thought and time to make good informed decisions. You are more likely to get what you want if you have a clear understanding of what that is. Working with a professional will help you determine what you want your financial future to look like after divorce.

Your financial situation is unique to you; take the time to figure out what you want for yourself. If you don't, someone else will figure it out for you and you may not like it in the end.

"The first year after our divorce, we tried to outdo one another with birthday gifts for our children, in essence, buying their love. Now I look at the kids' birthdays and am thankful that I can buy half as many gifts, knowing that they will get plenty of gifts from their friends and other family members."

REAL ESTATE ADVICE

KURT GROESSER, REALTOR ®, MBA

JAN PARSONS
SENIOR MORTGAGE BANKER

Kurt's Personal Story

In the summer of 1984, my parents decided on a trial separation and began divorce proceedings. My sister was thirteen years old and I was only seven, but I still have vivid memories of moving out of our home on Buttonwood Drive. My parents had been fighting for months and, in many ways, I was relieved to be in a new environment.

It was a small two-bedroom townhome on Strachan Drive and my father, sister, and I quickly made it our home. My sister and I still call it "the Strachan House" when we talk about that time. The floor plan was much smaller than our Buttonwood home and the yard was a postage stamp, but that didn't stop me from running around the small yard emulating the Olympians we watched in the summer games that year.

My father is a proud man and I have little doubt that renting "the Strachan House" after years of home ownership played on his ego. We were downsizing but we were regrouping—emotionally and financially. We lived there for a year before we settled again in a new home.

Ultimately, it didn't matter to my sister and me that we were living in a rental home. We just wanted things to get back to normal. Summer turned to fall and I enrolled in a new elementary school and found new friends. Our family survived and, fortunately, my parents were able to reconcile their differences that year without finalizing the divorce. I look back on that time at "the Strachan House" with a sense of great strength even though it was difficult.

I share this story with you for two reasons. First, don't assume that you have to immediately provide a "worthy replacement" to the marital home you and your children have known. Second, what your children need most is a sense of normalcy, and a transition home, like our "Strachan House," may be the best way to facilitate that.

Jan's Personal Story

After I divorced, I thought I needed to keep my son in the same type of neighborhood we were moving from — large upper-middle-class homes in nice, tidy cul-de-sac's. I immediately jumped into a new, large house with a big backyard. Even though my brother encouraged me NOT to purchase the new house, I was singing "I am Woman, hear me roar!" But I jumped right into the proverbial frying pan.

What I have learned in the last few years is that my dog, Hannah, large as she may be, is a house dog who loves being indoors with her family. My son LOVED living at his father's small, rented condominium. I, on the other hand, did NOT love caring for a large house and yard. I was incapable of giving my undivided attention to my son on the weekends because I was busy mowing, edging, weed-eating and cleaning.

After about a year of keeping up the maintenance, I was yearning for a nice smaller-sized townhome where someone else took care of the landscaping and snow blowing and I could concentrate on soccer and basketball with my son.

I also took out a large mortgage on my new home thinking that when I started back into the business world I would be hugely successful. What I failed to remember was that I had not worked in seven years and it was a bit more difficult getting back on my feet than I had anticipated. Not only was I yearning for a smaller home, but also a smaller mortgage.

By all means, if you have the financial strength to purchase the Taj Majal and hire a gardener and cleaning person, you have my blessing. But if you have an uncertain financial future like I had, it is best to play it safe. I now wish I had rented for a few months until my head was clear and I was thinking more logically instead of emotionally.

SHOULD WE SELL THE "MARITAL HOME"?

For most couples, the marital home is the most significant financial burden as well as the most significant asset in their portfolio. The decision to sell or not to sell can be an emotional rollercoaster and the main battleground in the divorce. In some situations, the divorce proceedings may require the sale of the home in order to divide the proceeds equitably. If neither spouse can afford to keep up the house payments alone, it will be in their best interest to sell as quickly as possible. Couples with children will have other considerations, such as whether or not to keep the home until the children finish school.

One of the first things you can do to help make your decision is to get an appraisal. Although many popular websites will offer an estimated value of your home, the information is often not accurate. Neither do you want to rely on the tax assessor's value of your home. Instead, get a Broker's Opinion of Value (BOV) or a Comparative Marketing Analysis (CMA) from a local real estate agent. Your attorney along with any professional involved in your divorce will need to get this information.

Keep in mind, the value of a house is ultimately determined by what a buyer is willing to pay for it and what you are willing to sell it for TODAY. Unfortunately, many people have preconceived notions of what their home is worth based on the "real estate bubble" in the mid to late 2000's. If you were not fortunate enough to sell your last home at its artificial peak during that time or if you bought your current home during that time, you may have lost some of your equity during the market correction. In order to sell your home as quickly as possible for the best price, you will need to know what the home is worth NOW.

If your home is worth less than what you currently owe, you have several options. First, one spouse may be able to keep the home until the market improves. Second, a loan modification may lower the payment to a manageable level. Third, you can rent the home until the market improves. Fourth, you may be able to negotiate a short sale of the home. In a short sale, a real estate agent will list your home for sale and market it to buyers just as they would in a normal sale. Once you receive an offer, the agent will negotiate a settlement with your bank to forgive the short fall or arrange for a reduced payment to settle the remaining debt. A short sale has important tax and legal consequences to the divorcing couple, so you will need to discuss this option carefully with both your CPA and attorney.

TIPS FOR SELLING YOUR HOME QUICKLY

The moment you place your home on the market you are entering a competition—a price war and a beauty contest. Winning homes will have the best value in both of these categories in the eyes of buyers. One of the most important questions you need to ask your realtor is: "How do we stack up against the competition?" Investors who regularly fix up and sell houses will make sure their properties have better curb appeal and more "bang for the buck" than comparable homes. A few things you can do include clearing the clutter, touching up paint, and hiring a realtor who uses a professional photographer.

TO PREPARE YOUR HOME FOR SALE

❖   Clean up the clutter, especially in the bathrooms and kitchen (remove unnecessary items and appliances from the countertops)

❖   Hire a handyman to finish projects and/or touch up paint inside and outside

❖   Have carpets and windows cleaned

❖   Hire a professional home stager

❖   Make sure your real estate agent uses a professional photographer for marketing

What do you do if your "spouse" does not comply? Unfortunately, it is quite common to have one spouse sabotage the efforts to sell the marital home. The courts can help to resolve disputes over the showing and staging of the home. If your soon-to-be-ex is causing problems with scheduled showings or leaving the home in disarray, talk to your attorney right away. You cannot afford to miss out on a buyer who is ready, willing and able to buy your home.

HIRING A
REAL ESTATE AGENT

You've made the difficult decision to sell the marital home; now it's time to pick the best real estate agent to sell it quickly for the best price possible. So who do you choose? Most of us know a friend, family member or acquaintance who "dabbles" in real estate, but if you want to make sure your home sells quickly this is NOT the time to hire your friend's mother's cousin to list your home. An experienced agent who knows the current economic situation and consistently sells homes faster than the average for your area is your best option.

Professional real estate agents will often be a member of the local board of Realtors® and will have access to marketing your property on the local board website, often called the MLS (multiple listing service). You will also want to consider interviewing several agents who have successfully sold homes in your neighborhood.

You may want to hire an agent who specializes in divorce (www.RealEstateDivorceSpecialist.com). Divorce proceedings can complicate the sale of a house if there are disagreements over the distribution of the marital assets or liens placed on the property. If you can't successfully complete the sale of your home after you've gone under contract with a buyer, the legal and financial ramifications could be very costly, depending on the laws in your state.

There are several questions to ask an agent when interviewing one to list your home, including if they work full-time, how long their houses are on the market, on average, and what do they do to market homes. If you and your "spouse" can't agree on a real estate agent, the courts may select one for you.

QUESTIONS TO ASK YOUR POTENTIAL REAL ESTATE AGENT

❖   Are you a full-time or part-time agent?

❖   What is the average number of days your listings are on the market before selling?

❖   What websites will my home be listed on?

❖   How quickly do you respond to phone calls?

❖   How often can I expect to hear from you concerning updates?

❖   What specifically do you do to market properties?

"I had previously been the sole owner of my home prior to my marriage. Upon divorce, I didn't realize that I only had to include the amount that the house had increased in value since the marriage as a 'marital asset.' I was so relieved to learn that this was the only part of the home that he was entitled to in the divorce."

OTHER REAL ESTATE ASSETS

Investment properties are important to consider in the division of marital assets. They may be rental property, vacation homes, time shares, or commercial real estate investments. The factors that distinguish an investment from a personal residence are related to ownership and use. If either spouse used the property as a personal residence in two of the last five years, the property may be considered a personal residence eligible for an exemption from capital gains taxes. On the other hand, investment properties are generally subject to capital gains taxes when sold. You will want to talk to your CPA and real estate agent about the benefits of a 1031 Exchange to defer your capital gains tax burden and roll your equity into a new investment property (see more on capital gains rules below).

Keep in mind that a property deeded in one person's name can be sold prior to the divorce proceedings without the consent of the other spouse. After the divorce begins, the courts may issue an injunction that prevents the sale of properties while the divorce is proceeding. Also, a "lis pendens" order may be used to further diminish the chances of a spouse selling a property during a divorce. The order is publicly recorded with the county and indicates to any prospective buyer that there is a court proceeding that could prevent the clean sale of the property while the title to the property is "clouded." A "lis pendens" is very effective but it also requires a court order to be removed; you will not be able to sell the property until it is fully removed from the title.

Depending on the laws of your state, there may be specific rules that dictate the division of marital property. Marital property refers to any property purchased by either spouse during the marriage up to the time of the final divorce decree. Property that was inherited or gifted to either spouse and held in separate title is treated differently. In many cases, the appreciation in value of properties from the time they were received is considered marital property. Properties owned by a spouse's business might also be considered marital property.

It may not be necessary to sell all (or any) of the marital properties to divide real estate assets. In fact, if the properties are appreciating in value, it may be beneficial to keep the properties until they achieve a higher value. Properties can be deeded from one spouse to another with a "quit claim deed" by a lawyer or title company. This transfer is a quick and relatively simple way to divide the marital property and it has no tax consequence to either spouse. When a property is later sold, however, it will likely be subject to capital gains taxes. Be sure to talk to a CPA and financial planner about the latest tax rules relating to the sale of investment properties.

CAPITAL GAINS TAXES

Over the years the US Tax code has allowed homeowners to waive a portion of their capital gains on the value of their personal residences. In order for a home to be considered a personal residence, there are ownership and use criteria that must be satisfied.

As of 2010, your home is considered a personal residence if you have owned it for at least five years and have used it as your home address for at least two of those years. Currently, married couples are eligible to use a $500,000 capital gains tax exemption on the sale of a personal residence. Single people are eligible for a $250,000 capital gains tax exemption.

For a divorced couple, there are special rules that allow both spouses to individually receive the $250,000 tax exemption on their marital home, even years after the fact. If your "spouse" received the home in the divorce settlement, you may still qualify for the exemption once the home is sold. To be eligible, however, you will need to remain on the title to the home, so plan carefully at the start of the divorce. Either party can use their "spouse's" use of the home for two of five years for the eligibility requirement. Obviously, this can be complicated, so you will want to consult with a lawyer, financial planner, and CPA to set the scenario up correctly from the start.

YOUR NEXT HOME

The divorce is final, the marital home has sold and you are left to decide whether to purchase a home or rent. First, DO NOT compete with your "spouse." Don't give in to perceived pressure from your children or elsewhere to replace the big house. Next, don't make competitive jabs in the years after the divorce by trying to outdo your "spouse" with homes and/or property. Instead, talk to a financial planner to develop a new vision to achieve your personal goals and use that plan to direct your decisions. A costly real estate mistake can be difficult to undo.

THINK BEFORE YOU BUY

Think twice before single-handedly taking on more than you can chew. You may think that you, your children and the family dog need a large house with a large yard, but be very careful what you wish for. The upkeep of a large home is enormous and overwhelming when you are trying to work a full-time job and care for your children as a single parent.

If the marital home has not been sold, you may wish to stay in it for the children or yourself. This may be a wise decision if you can financially accomplish it. However, it will need to be refinanced if both you and your "spouse" are on the note and/or loan. Your income will likely be cut so you should consult a mortgage professional to find out if refinancing is feasible.

You may be surprised what a mortgage professional can do for you. You may qualify for a loan when you don't have much to put down, which is preferable to renting for a long period of time. Or you may need expert testimony in court stating you can afford to refinance on your own and buy-out your "spouse." Bottom line: Contact a mortgage professional to see what options are out there now or in your future with proper planning.

MORTGAGE 101

You have found a new home or possibly a vacation home in the mountains or near the ocean. Perhaps you would like to own investment property and become a landlord. These are all different types of properties and the interest rates will vary according.

Let's start with your primary residence. Before you begin shopping for a new home, it is important to contact a mortgage professional to both know what price range you can afford and get pre-qualified. Keep in mind that getting pre-qualified does not mean that you will absolutely qualify. It just means that you have gone through the preliminary stages of the pre-qualification process. You have been pre-qualified, NOT pre-approved.

A loan officer will ask you several questions. A main one: "What does your credit look like?" Have a copy of your credit report handy so you are familiar with your credit score as well as what debt shows on your report. Another question: "What is your income?" Know your earnings, either annually or monthly. Next: "What are your assets?" These include a 401K, an IRA, stocks, etc.

Also, if you either receive or pay child or spousal support, you must disclose this to your loan officer. Your divorce decree must state that you will be receiving child/spousal support for at least three years for a lender to accept it as income.

Your mortgage professional will also need to know how much you plan on putting down and how long you plan on living in your new home. Perhaps this is a transitional home or maybe it is the home you plan on never leaving. Once your loan officer has all your information and has discussed your long-term financial goals, they will go to work to see if you qualify to purchase a home. There are several different loan programs and they should be willing to show you all your options.

Once your loan officer has determined the price range you can afford and has you pre-qualified, the fun begins. It's time to call your real estate agent. It's also time to introduce your mortgage professional to your agent. They will be working together. Your realtor will need to ask your loan officer for a "pre-approval letter." This basically states that you have been pre-qualified for a loan in a certain price range. When you find a home and make an offer, this document will be given to the listing realtor. When your offer gets accepted, you and your loan officer will get to work to obtain a mortgage. There are some basic documents they will need from you such as a copy of your driver's license, pay stubs and a divorce decree, among many others. They will submit these with your loan application.

> *"When I went through divorce, I got so focused on the negative aspects of my former spouse that I forgot all the positives. It took years for me to risk seeing the positive again; however, once I did this, I found that I was happier, our interactions were less stressful and it opened the door to a more friendly future between the two of us."*

DOCUMENTS TO SUBMIT WITH YOUR LOAN APPLICATION

❖   Signed purchase contract

❖   Copy of your driver's license and Social Security card

❖   Evidence that you are obtaining homeowner's insurance

❖   Signed loan documents (your lender will prepare these once you have a contract on your home)

❖   W-2's or tax returns if you are self-employed

❖   Pay stubs

❖   Checking and savings account statements

❖   Asset statements

❖   Divorce decree if applicable

PARTS OF YOUR MONTHLY PAYMENT

PITI: Principal, interest, taxes and insurance

Principle: The overall principle is the amount you borrowed and are charged interest on. The monthly principle is the amount actually being deducted from the overall principle. This amount goes up over time.

Interest: The overall interest is the amount that borrowing the principle is costing you (along with the loan fees). The monthly interest is the interest cost for that month. This amount goes down over time.

Taxes: Property taxes vary according to the county you live in and are determined monthly by dividing your annual assessment by twelve months.

Insurance: The mortgage lender will require you to obtain homeowner's insurance to cover your home against theft, fire and natural disasters.

HOA Dues: HOA (home owner's association) dues will not become part of your mortgage payment, but the monthly amount will be included to ensure you can pay your HOA dues.

LET'S TALK CREDIT

Your credit score and debt are important pieces to a complicated puzzle. A potential lender will need to pull your credit from three different credit reporting bureaus. Most often, your "mid-FICO* score" is what determines your interest rate along with qualifying you for a loan: the higher the score, the better the interest rate. It's a good idea to obtain your own credit score first so you can correct any inaccuracies. It's not uncommon for there to be errors.

It's also not a bad thing to carry some debt. The rule of thumb is to not have more than 30% of your available credit charged on any loan. Keep to that and make your payments on time and your credit should stay in good shape.

WHAT YOUR FICO CREDIT SCORE MEANS

If your score is less than 620, you currently will not be pre-approved for a home mortgage.

If your score is 620 to 680, you may qualify for an FHA loan.

If your score is 680 and above, you may qualify for a conventional loan.

If your score is 720 and above, you will qualify for a loan with the best rates available at that time

* FICO stands for Fair, Isaac and Company, the company that historically assigned credit ratings.

Negative factors that may have lowered your FICO credit score include closing accounts, moving often, high balance on credit cards and charge-offs. If your credit is not in the best shape, do not despair. It is always repairable. Your mortgage professional should be able to guide you in the right direction for improving your credit score.

"The best advice I got during my divorce was to take the high road, grin and bare it and never badmouth my former spouse. This has paid off in spades. It kept me from exposing my 'dirty laundry' to the neighborhood, and it kept my children safe from nasty comments and discussions about their parents' divorce. It also made it easier to eventually be friendly with my ex."

MORTGAGE PRODUCTS AVAILABLE

30-YEAR FIXED:

The 30-year fixed mortgage is the most common product out there today. With this type of mortgage, your loan will stay unchanged throughout the life of the loan. If you plan on living in your home for many years, this is your bet.

ADJUSTABLE-RATE MORTGAGE:

With an adjustable-rate mortgage, the interest rate will vary depending on if you choose a three, five, seven or ten-year adjustable-rate mortgage. The interest rate will be lower than a 30-year fixed loan, but it will adjust when your term is up. This product works if you know you will only be in your home for three to ten years. Let's say you have a daughter who is in tenth grade and will be graduating in two years and going away to college. Perhaps you will want to downsize then or retire near your family. This product makes good financial sense if you are CERTAIN you will be selling soon. But you don't want to get stuck with a higher interest rate should you stay.

FHA (Federal Housing Administration):

If you have a minimal amount of savings for a down payment, an FHA loan is the product for you.

You can choose from a 30-year fixed or an adjustable-rate mortgage. An FHA loan also allows for a less-than-stellar credit score. As long as you have a 620 mid-FICO score or higher, FHA is willing to lend to you.

Current guidelines require you put down 3.5% of the purchase price. You will also need mortgage insurance which helps guarantee your repayment of the loan. If you do not have 3.5% to put down on a home, there are several "down payment assistance programs." Some require as little as $500 down and many will defer the payments for several years and or have very low interest rates attached to them.

Bottom line: Consult with your mortgage professional to find a program that fits your needs. The process of obtaining a mortgage may seem a bit intimidating, but it is well worth the outcome once you are given the keys to YOUR new home.

"*My best support systems were my closest friends and family members. I was careful not to rely on my children for support. I had watched my neighbor depend on her kids for emotional support during her divorce and her kids were practically raising her.*"

EMOTIONAL SUPPORT AND PARENTING PLANS

KRISTINE TURNER, PH.D.

Kristine's Personal Story

I went to graduate school, got my degree as a clinical psychologist, got married, bought a house, and had children in my twenties. In my thirties, I unexpectedly got a divorce. I mistakenly believed that my years of experience as a psychologist and facilitator of parenting after divorce classes would make the process easier. Unfortunately, I forgot to calculate the depth of emotional factors that would play into the whole ordeal.

Initially, I thought we could settle the divorce in an amicable manner. After a few failed attempts, it became clear that both of us would need to hire attorneys to help us through the process. I didn't interview attorneys, which was a big mistake, going with the first one someone recommended. I didn't like working with her and dreaded every interaction we had, not to mention paying the bill each month.

As the case wore on, I became physically and emotionally exhausted. Although divorce was our solution to the marital problems, it became a problem unto itself. The more time we spent with attorneys, the less we talked to each other, and the more we came to distrust and dislike the other person. Neither of us was getting our needs met, and both of us were fostering a "fear factor."

Our limited conversations left us frustrated and hurt and we lacked the tools to reach a settlement on our own. If we had been forced into mediation, as many states now require, we might have resolved our differences in a meaningful way. A third party in the room would have helped us fight for a settlement rather than fight each other.

Instead, we continued down our war path, locked into our various positions, getting our families and friends to see our sides. Our divorce became the talk of the neighborhood—how embarrassing. In the end, it took more than a year to finalize our divorce but that wasn't the end of the story. Although I was satisfied with the results, my "spouse" was not. His needs hadn't been adequately addressed.

So a few years later, he filed motions for modifications to parenting time, followed by motions for modifications for child support. I just wanted him to "leave me alone" and he wanted justice. After another year or two of hiring CFI's (child and family investigators) and finding new attorneys to represent us, we received another set of court orders. This time, I felt my needs weren't met and I paid dearly (emotionally, physically and financially) for this unpleasant experience.

Hopefully, the wisdom in the pages of this book can prevent you from going down a long, tiresome, less-than-rewarding path towards divorce. Many couples find ways to divorce in a manner that meets their financial and parental needs, as well as the emotional need to preserve their dignity and well-being during what can be a grueling process. I hope this latter path can become the one that you follow.

NOBODY PLANS TO DIVORCE

Currently half of all marriages end in divorce. Yet we don't plan to divorce, so few of us have much information about the better and worse paths to traverse during a divorce. We essentially have to learn "on the fly" as we are going through the process. I certainly didn't decide to add divorce to my "bucket list" of things I wanted to accomplish in life. However, I did get to experience divorce (twice as a matter of fact), and as I put my own teachings into practice, I gained a new appreciation for what works in theory and what works in reality. In this section of the book, I will share with you what works and why it works, as well as what you can do to lessen the negative impact of divorce while simultaneously strengthening the positive.

There's so much talk about the negative aspects of divorce. I wish we heard more about the positive. If a family successfully manages a divorce, the children can walk away from the experience as stronger, more capable people. On the other hand, when a couple stays in a high-conflict marriage, the "ice wars" can be more damaging to their children than solving the problem via divorce. Not only does divorce reduce the conflict, it allows parents to reach their full potential as individuals because they cease putting so much time and energy into a marriage that isn't working. In turn, they are able to put more time and energy into their children.

Your Support System

One of the most important things you can do is establish a support system for yourself. If there's a silver lining to the fact that half of marriages currently choose divorce, it's that there's more and more support for individuals going through this transition. If your venue is self-help books, there are plenty to choose from. One of my favorites is Bruce Fisher's *Rebuilding, When Your Relationship Ends*.

If you like therapy or coaching, plenty of counselors specialize in helping families get through the divorce process. Coaching people through the pathways of divorce has become a popular alternative to traditional counseling. It focuses more specifically on how to traverse the paths of divorce as opposed to gaining insight and in-depth understanding about what makes you tick. Having someone to talk to who can provide wisdom around both the emotional and physical aspects of divorce can be invaluable as you work towards rebuilding your life.

Friends and family can also offer a significant support system as can groups and classes which focus on surviving the divorce process. It is essential that you find a support system that works for you, not only for yourself but for your children. In essence, you will be their role model; you have the opportunity to demonstrate how to handle massive changes in life and cope with strong emotions. Plus if you are taking care of yourself, you will be better equipped to take care of your children and their needs.

TELLING YOUR CHILDREN ABOUT THE DIVORCE

Both parents need to tell their children about the divorce; re-telling the story is okay. Repeat the following message to them from time to time:

Divorce Is Final

It was an Adult Decision

It was Not Their Fault

Reassure them you are available and there for them. Children often wonder, "Can parents divorce me, too?" You need to make it clear to them that parents don't divorce their children. Provide an area or situation in which their voice is heard. This lets them know they matter. "Kids need their say, not necessarily their way."

LETTING YOUR CHILDREN EXPRESS THEIR FEELINGS

Believe it or not, most parents only spend one and a half minutes per day actively listening to their children. Most of our time is spent giving instructions: "Set the table"; "Brush your teeth"; "Get into bed"; and so on. Try to become an active listener. Allow your children the time and freedom to express their feelings. Do not be afraid to ask about their negative feelings. Let them know that all their feelings are okay.

One of my favorite things I did with my children involved our bedtime routine. A couple of evenings a week, when I was putting them to bed, I would check in with them to see how they were coping with the divorce. I liked talking to them in the evenings because it was quiet and there weren't too many pressures on our time. Ask your children: "What was your high point today?" and "What was your low point today?" These kinds of questions can elicit conversation and often lead to helpful discussions.

Some families may prefer to have discussions around the dinner table, while others feel that car rides present good opportunities to discuss the divorce. Children often prefer the car because they don't have to look you in the eye; they are seated behind or next to you. Regardless of the method you choose, make sure that you build some time into your schedule to check in with you children on a regular basis.

And be careful not to make this time about you. Try not to "parentify" your children—don't make them your friend. They need to be your children and you need to be the parent. They need to know that they can depend on you for support, and that they don't need to take care of you. Your support should come from other adults and other sources.

❖ ❖ ❖

TIP

NEVER try to get support from your children. They may try to be your friend out of their fear of abandonment, but in the end it will only confuse them. Children need to know that they can turn to you for support, not the other way around.

GIVING YOUR CHILDREN ROUTINE AND CONSISTENCY

Provide your children with routine, consistency and dependability. As soon as you can, re-establish family rituals such as "Wednesday is pizza night." Play board or video games with them, watch their favorite TV shows together or read aloud from their favorite books. Routine gives children a sense of control and power in a healthy way.

This turned out to be my favorite part of the divorce. Once I got through the loss, I realized that I got to pick and choose all the activities at my house, with my children's input, of course. I found that I really didn't like some of the things we had been doing as a family such as fishing. I would leave that and camping and boating for their dad. We go to museums and travel to national parks (without the camping).

Another plus has been my parents' involvement. Now that I am single, they can come and go without causing any marital rift. My children get to see their grandparents on a regular basis, and I have a better bond my parents. In essence, we have two generations providing wisdom while raising the children.

Try to spend your time with the children instilling your values and priorities. You need to be dependable. Say what you mean and mean what you say (but don't say it mean). In short, do what you say you are going to do. You are your children's role model. The healthier emotionally you are, the more consistent you are at managing your new life, the better off your children will be as they work through this family transition.

FOOLS RUSH IN

Humans are social beings. There is a biological pull that many of us feel towards living with other people. It is tough to deny ourselves the bonds that cohabitation affords. We need others for support and nurturance. So it may not surprise you that around 85% of people go on to remarry within three to five years post their divorce.

What most of us do is remarry the same kind of person we just divorced. They have a different name and face, but the personality traits are similar. Something in your childhood or personality attracts you to certain types of people and you will usually continue that pattern unless you make a conscious attempt to alter it.

One way to do this is to develop your own "new IDENTITY." Allow yourself the gift of time, at least a couple of years to heal and rebuild your life. Learn about yourself before you start dating again; ask yourself tough questions: "Why was I attracted to my former spouse?"; "What worked in the marriage? Why?"; "What didn't work? Why?"; "What type of person am I better suited to be around?"; "What types of people are better for me to associate with? Why?"

By asking yourself these types of questions, you gain a better understanding about your relationship choices and why your choice in spouse ultimately didn't work out. You will also learn more about what you had hoped the marriage would fulfill for you. Can it be fulfilled without remarriage? Do you really want to remarry? Is dating without worrying about remarriage a better alternative for you?

As a psychologist who taught parenting after divorce classes, I thought I had it all figured out. When I went through my first divorce, I had been contemplating the problems for a couple of years. I thought I had done a lot of the healing work and thus made the mistake of quickly seeking comfort in a new relationship.

We have this natural tendency to want intimate connection, but we really need to give ourselves plenty of time to heal from one relationship before we get too serious about another. If I could do it all over again, I would date more people or simply go out with good friends and try new activities or hobbies. I would take the time to heal and learn from my past mistakes before rushing into a new marriage.

FIVE BASIC
EMOTIONAL STAGES

There are five basic emotional stages to divorce (similar to the stages of grief) and you will need to go through them if you want to heal yourself.

DENIAL:

Denial is the initial period of not accepting the reality of the divorce or loss. It is a natural defense that allows you enough time to accept what is happening. You may feel numb or in shock. You may say for instance, "This can't be happening to me or my family." Children may find themselves saying, "My mom's not gone; she's on a business trip."

ANGER:

Anger is an intense feeling of rage, envy or resentment and may be targeted at innocent bystanders, such as your children. You may feel angry about being let down and you may act out feelings in a variety of inappropriate ways. Finding an acceptable way to express your anger is an integral part of the healing process.

Notice I said "acceptable" because anger is normal in a divorce. What you do with your anger is the key. Do you exercise, take time out or call a friend? Or do you yell and scream, use substances or punch holes in walls?

During the anger stage, you will find yourself more focused on your "spouse's" faults—blaming the other person as opposed to looking at your own negative and positive contributions to the marriage. Remember, you are your children's role model; they will emulate what they see you doing.

BARGAINING:

Bargaining is a period of wanting to fix things that are beyond your control. It's rethinking your decision to divorce. You might say something like, "If only I had done such and such..." You may feel guilt for what has happened and may blame yourself. Your children may think the divorce is their fault and act really good or really bad in order to take the attention off of the divorce. If they get the attention, they assume you will get back together. Let them know that the divorce is not their fault. It was an adult decision.

DEPRESSION:

Depression occurs when the reality of the loss sets in. At this stage, you may feel despair. You may question your ability to deal with your sadness and turn to unhealthy coping devices to ease your pain: overeating, sleep disorders, excessive alcohol consumption and drug use are all manifestations of a depressed state.

Instead, you need nurturing, self-care, and healthy ways to live with your sadness to overcome any unrealistic guilt you may feel. This stage also gives you an opportunity to learn a lot about yourself: "What did you bring to the marriage?"; "What aspects of the divorce were your contributions?"; "What can you learn about yourself because of this relationship?"

ACCEPTANCE:

Acceptance is the final emotional stage of divorce or grief. It is a time when change is no longer a threat. It may even be welcome. Depending on your circumstances, you might be more accepting of your present circumstances or more optimistic about your future. In any case, you have lived through and survived a difficult time, but it has passed and life does go on.

> "The best advice I got during my divorce was to focus on the only thing that I could control, myself. It was hard to realize that I couldn't control my former spouse or my kids' reaction to the divorce. The only person I could control was me."

KEY POINTS TO REMEMBER

PARENTS CAN BE IN DIFFERENT EMOTIONAL STAGES:

Going through these five emotional stages is a necessary process towards healing that may or may not go in the exact order listed above. So parents may not be in the same stage as each other. Children, however, always follow their parents through the stages; in other words, children cannot get to acceptance unless one of their parents does.

Sometimes one parent will get stuck in the anger stage. Anger is a secondary emotion that masks pain and sadness underneath. A person might be unwilling to experience sadness and fight to suppress it by staying angry, undermining any attempt to heal after a divorce. So it is vital that you make every attempt to heal yourself.

YOU SHOULD NEVER CRITICIZE THE OTHER PARENT:

Never criticize the other parent in front of your children. Because children see themselves as extensions of their parents, they often feel like you are criticizing them when you badmouth the other parent. I am often asked in my seminars how you can overcome a situation where the other parent is badmouthing you. Nobody wants to roll over and take it, especially from their "spouse."

The option I like best is to tell your children that you have a different viewpoint or opinion than the other parent. Make sure that you don't badmouth them in the process; simply say that you see things differently and that having different opinions is perfectly normal. Then your children are free to choose how to interpret the situation

Although children need to know that the divorce wasn't their fault, they don't need to know all the juicy details about why you chose to divorce. Don't tell children too many adult specifics about the divorce. It's better to say, "Mom and Dad aren't happy as husband and wife, and we want to put our energy into raising you instead of into the marriage. We think that this will help our family."

I realize that some of you feel like the divorce was not your choice. Divorce is usually easier when both parties want it, but on the flip side, you can't force someone to stay in a marriage when they want out. It won't lead to "happily ever after." In this case, you may struggle with what to say to your children. It's perfectly okay to say that you and your "spouse" wanted to solve the marital problems in different ways (you wanted counseling while he wanted a divorce); however, the end result is still divorce. The trick to saying this is to do it without badmouthing the other parent.

On a positive note, it is "music to their ears" when you say something nice about the other parent. Let your children know that you want them to love both parents and that you aren't going to get in the way of them having a loving relationship with Mom or Dad. Another tact might be to say to your "spouse" (in the most loving way possible) something like, "I read a book that says it's not helpful to speak negatively about your former spouse in front of the children; I am going to practice this approach. Children need to love both of their parents and I intend to help foster that love."

LIMIT YOUR CHILDREN'S EXPOSURE TO CONFLICT:

Limit conflict at all costs. Familial conflict is one of the most damaging things we can do to our children. Nothing is worse for children than to witness their parents fighting in the driveway during a change in custody. If you think that you will fight, try to arrange for someone else to make the exchange or try using a neutral location as an alternative, such as school or daycare.

When you are dropping your children off with the other parent versus picking them up, take advantage of it. Send a subtle but important message by "giving" them to the other parent versus the other parent "taking" them away. Say something like, "Tell your dad 'hi' for me," or "Don't forget to give Dad the special treat we bought for him."

AVOID PARENTAL LOSS

The children who rarely see Mom or never see Dad after the divorce suffer tremendously. They grow up feeling incomplete, constantly wondering why their mom or dad doesn't want to spend time with them. It can lead to abandonment issues, relationship problems and low self-esteem well into their adult years, even causing them to pass on their difficulties to their children.

You may feel like using your "spouse's" behavior as a weapon to keep them from the children, even fight to deny them any parental rights. Unless the situation is extreme having to do with criminal activity or abusive actions, spare your children the loss of the other parent. But if the other parent has a drinking problem, for example, there are options to protect your children while allowing them to see Mom or Dad. Perhaps the court order can state your "spouse" cannot drive with the children in the car or cannot be with the children alone.

If you are in a situation where the other parent is absent by choice, all is not lost, but you will have to pick up some of the pieces. Let your children know that the divorce is not their fault and that their absent parent does love them: "Mom or Dad is not in a position to do much caretaking right now," or "Mom or Dad is working on healing before getting back into parenting again." By saying these things, you are helping your children see that they are still lovable, that the issues are not about them.

PARENTING PLANS

Developing a parenting plan is an essential part of the divorce process. It is important that children get plenty of access to each of their parents.

If both parents have been active and involved before the divorce, a more equal division of parenting time can occur. In situations where one parent has done the majority of the childcare, that parent should continue to be the primary parent until the children have time to adapt to spending more time with the secondary parent. Then, over time, it is feasible for the children to spend 50% of their time with each parent.

Keep in mind that the younger your children are, the harder it is for them to be away from a parent (particularly a primary parent) for long periods of time. Sometimes shorter, more frequent exchanges are helpful. As children get older, they can tolerate longer stays away from a parent. If siblings are going from Mom's house to Dad's house together, this makes the transitions easier for them. Younger children will often tolerate a more lengthy stay away from a parent if they have siblings with them. As children reach their "tween" and teen years, they are much more capable of a 50% parenting split.

Some parents prefer a week with the children and a week without. The positive aspect this plan offers is fewer transitions; families can settle into a routine for a longer period of time. The downside is the longer breaks children have from their parents. Consider that children's sense of time is quite different from an adult's. A week might rush by for you, but your child might think it's an eternity.

Another popular plan is a 5-2-2-5 plan where one parent has the kids on Monday and Tuesday, the other parent has the children on Wednesday and Thursday, and then Friday, Saturday and Sunday are alternated between Mom's house and Dad's house. This plan has consistency, but more transitions between households. It does, however, keep both parents involved in the children's lives on a weekly if not daily basis.

There are an infinite number of possible plans that might work for your family. Jobs, schools and other factors will have to be taken into account when developing your parenting plan.

Bottom line: Find a plan that works for the whole family—one in which your children can thrive.

Remember that you can still participate in your children's lives even when they aren't staying at your house. Go to their sporting events, practices, plays and rehearsals; volunteer at their school; call them on a regular basis; and send text messages or emails. Continue to build the relationship with them that you have always wanted.

> *"I try to say positive things about the kids' dad on occasion. It seems to be music to their ears, and it really reduces my negative feelings toward him."*

PARENTING CLASSES

PARENTING AFTER DIVORCE CLASSES:

In many states, courts mandate that divorcing parents attend a co-parenting after divorce class, often needing to see a certificate of completion. These classes are typically four hours long and focus on the best interest of the child.

Basically, these classes cover the positive and negative approaches to co-parenting after a divorce. They discourage things like badmouthing your "spouse" in front of the children and encourage being flexible and cooperative with each another.

(Online Class: www.NewBeginningsCoParenting.com)

HIGH-CONFLICT PARENTING CLASSES:

Many states also offer "level two" parenting classes for high-conflict cases. They can run from eight to twelve weeks, meeting weekly for an hour or two.

These classes tend to focus on co-parenting from a parallel approach, which is how to parent as individuals thereby minimizing the interaction between parents. These classes also point out the damage that can be done to children if the conflict between parents persists through the years.

USEFUL TIPS TO HELP YOUR CHILDREN

❖   Reassure your children that they will continue to have a relationship with both parents.

❖   Reassure your children that you will be available to them.

❖   Demonstrate your love on a daily basis.

❖   Show your children through your actions that you are trustworthy.

❖   Continue to set limits and discipline your children because structure is helpful to them.

❖   Listen to your children. Spend 20 minutes a day sitting quietly with your children, allowing them to talk about their day and their feelings. Make eye contact with them. Do not offer advice unless they ask for it.

❖   Encourage children to express their opinions.

❖   Encourage children to express their feelings (including sadness, loss, hurt, anger, guilt, helplessness or fear) even if what they say is hard to bear.

❖ Explain changes in concrete terms. Show them where each parent will live; reassure them that there will be enough food and money. Don't bother them with the details; refrain from sharing concerns about finances or residences with them.

❖ Keep children out of the middle.

❖ Help children adapt to both of their homes, for example, giving them a toothbrush, clothes, toys and books at both places.

❖ Communicate with the other parent about the children's issues.

❖ Develop a workable parenting plan that keeps both parents involved in their children's lives.

"Reduce the conflict! This was the best advice I got during my divorce. I tried hard to do my part in reducing the fighting, looking for settlement options and maintaining my sanity."

ABOUT THE DIVORCE TEAM

(from left to right)

DAVID W. HECKENBACH, ESQ.
JAN PARSONS, MORTGAGE BANKER
KRISTINE TURNER, PH.D.
KIM LANGELAAR, CDFA™
KURT GROESSER, REALTOR ®, MBA

DAVID W. HECKENBACH, ESQ.

Dave Heckenbach is a founding partner of Heckenbach Ammarell, LLP, which has been featured by *Forbes* magazine. His practice is primarily in the area of complicated divorce matters for individuals of high net worth and income. He has handled literally hundreds of contested hearings in cases involving divorce, paternity, allocation of parental responsibilities, post-decree modifications, child support modification, child support enforcement, maintenance modification, step-parent rights, and grandparent rights.

A trial lawyer for over 30 years specializing in complex litigation, Dave is best known as a formidable adversary in the courtroom, for his strategic abilities, and for the respect he commands from other attorneys and the judges. He has earned the title of "Super Lawyer" since that process began a number of years ago and has achieved that stature every consecutive year since. As such he is recognized by his peers as being in the top 5% of all attorneys in his community.

Dave is also known for his charity work, having been recognized as the top fundraiser for a Leukemia benefit and recipient of the Pacemaker award. He served on the board of the Alzheimer's Association, Cross and Clef ministries, and the American Heart Association of Colorado, for which he was board chairman and co-chairman for the Toyota celebrity ski challenge. He has also been listed in the Denver Social Register and Record since 1993.

Dave earned his Bachelor of Arts from Washington and Lee University in 1976, graduating cum laude with honors in Psychology (Psi Chi, the National Honors Society for Psychology). He received his Juris Doctorate from the University of Colorado School of Law in May, 1979.

KIM LANGELAAR, CDFA™

Kim Langelaar is a certified divorce financial analyst from the Institute of Divorce Financial Analyst as well as a trained mediator with almost a decade experience working in the financial and insurance field. Her training focuses on the tax and financial planning issues that face divorcing couples. She has taken advanced courses in alternative dispute resolution and her skills include helping couples communicate effectively in a highly emotional atmosphere. Kim's services include providing financial illustrations, projections for equitable distribution, lifestyle analysis, asset analysis, mediation, and court testimony.

After going through her own divorce fifteen years ago, Kim became passionate about helping others find better solutions to their divorces. She knows firsthand that divorce can get expensive and complicated. She understands the emotional difficulty a couple feels when ending their marriage. Her approach is to help them come to a fair agreement with integrity and respect.

Kim is a radio co-host for *New Beginnings, Life After Divorce* at Castle Rock Radio (www.CastleRockRadio.com). She is a member of the Metro Denver Interdisciplinary Committee, Financial Planning Association, and Institute for Divorce Financial Analysts. She holds a Bachelor's degree in Technical Management from DeVry University. She is licensed in health, life, auto, home, and commercial insurance with a Series 6, 63 and 65 securities license.

Kim lives with her three sons in Parker, Colorado. In her free time, she enjoys hiking, traveling and spending time with family and friends.

KURT GROESSER, REALTOR ®, MBA

Kurt Groesser has been involved in the real estate industry since 2003. He has experience in commercial real estate sales, property management, commercial leasing and residential real estate sales both as a principal and a broker.

In 2006, Kurt enhanced his skills when he graduated from Texas A&M University with an MBA. He holds a Bachelor's degree in marketing from the University of Colorado.

Kurt has been a licensed real estate broker in the State of Colorado since 2008. As an owner of commercial real estate and a broker, Kurt brings solid financial skills and practical experience to the real estate sales and investing process.

JAN PARSONS
SENIOR MORTGAGE BANKER

Jan Parsons has five years of mortgage loan experience specializing in assisting couples facing divorce. She has found that those who are going through divorce have particular needs and often a high degree of anxiety about keeping their current home or financing a new one. Having gone through a divorce herself, Jan understands how difficult it is to make educated decisions at such an emotional time.

As a Senior Mortgage Banker, Jan has the ability to lend in all 50 states. She has been an expert witness on a number of divorce cases and has amassed many hours of Continuing Legal Education in divorce law and the entire divorce process. Jan is a member of the Parker Chamber of Commerce and the Metro Denver Interdisciplinary Committee. In addition, she is a co-host of *New Beginnings, Life After Divorce*, a radio show for couples and families facing divorce (www.CastleRockRadio.com).

A longtime resident of Denver, Colorado, Jan is a single parent who enjoys spending time with her son, gardening, skiing, traveling, entertaining and volunteering for the Special Olympics.

KRISTINE TURNER, PH.D.

Kristine Turner graduated with a Ph.D. in clinical psychology from the Pacific Graduate School of Psychology, an APA accredited school affiliated with Stanford's program. She has worked since 1994 as a clinician in a wide variety of arenas including emergency services, group and individual therapy, leadership training, parental coaching, mediation and parenting after divorce classes for the courts. She has also appeared in court as an expert witness.

Kristine's primary passion is parenting after divorce—helping families traverse the rocky road of divorce, preparing countless parenting plans and performing personality evaluations and IQ tests for courts, mental health centers, schools and families going through divorce. As a divorced parent herself, her efforts have been focused on educating families about the better and worse paths to divorce.

Kristine practices in South Metro Denver, Colorado, and teaches weekly seminars, runs an on-line course for parents going through divorce, and appears regularly on TV Channel 2's *Everyday Show* and Douglas County's TV Channel 8. She also hosts her own radio show for families going through divorce, *New Beginnings, Life After Divorce* (www.CastleRockRadio.com). In addition, Kristine teaches high school leadership classes as well as leads anti-bullying summits in Douglas County.

Kristine is a member of the American Psychological Association, the Colorado Psychological Association and the Colorado Interdisciplinary Committee (formerly the MDICCC), an organization for mental health and legal professionals who deal with divorce-related issues. She also works with numerous county agencies and served as an elected official on her local school board for six years in Douglas County, Colorado.

Kristine has written two books on the subject of helping parents help their children cope with divorce: *Mommy and Daddy are Getting Divorced* (2010) and the *New Beginnings for Divorcing Parents Workbook*.

RECOMMENDED READING

BOOKS TO HELP YOU NAVIGATE THE DIVORCE PROCESS

ALL BOOKS AVAILABLE ON WWW.DIVORCEADVICE360.COM

Mom's House, Dad's House   **Issolina Ricci**
This book provides parents and children with an overview of what life looks like in two separate households. It includes suggestions for parenting plans and co-parenting arrangements broken down by age group and developmental stage.
ISBN: 0743277120

It's Not Your Fault, Koko Bear **Vicki Lansky**
This book follows the story of Koko Bear through the emotional stages of divorce. **ISBN: 0916773477**

Parents Are Forever   Shirley Thomas

This book is helpful to parents who are newly separated and gives a broad overview of what families can expect during the divorce process.

ISBN: 0964637839

Rebuilding, When Your Relationship Ends
Bruce Fisher

This book gives insight into rebuilding emotionally after divorce. The typical stages of grief are highlighted as well as coping mechanisms and techniques for regaining control after divorce.

ISBN: 1886230692

Dinosaurs Divorce   Marc Brown and
Laurene Krasny Brown

One of the first books ever written for children going through divorce, this remains a classic for younger children whose parents are divorcing.

ISBN: 0316109967

The Boys and Girls Book about Divorce
Richard Gardner, M.D.

This guide is written for older children ('tweens and teens). It discusses the emotions around divorce and what to do with them. It provides productive coping mechanisms for older children to use when they are angry or sad.   **ISBN: 0553276190**

Let's Talk About It: Divorce   Fred Rogers

Written by *Mr. Rogers* himself, this book on divorce uses photographs to depict the typical feelings and questions a child might have as the family goes through divorce.   **ISBN: 0698116704**

My Family's Changing   Pat Thomas

This is a practical guide for younger children about what to expect when their parents decide to divorce. Questions are inserted throughout the book to help children express their feelings.   **ISBN: 0764109952**

Mommy and Daddy are Getting Divorced
Kristine Turner, Ph.D.

In this read-along-with-your-children book, all the aspects of divorce are explained in an easy-to-understand way. Children will understand better what impact the divorce will have on their lives and even though they will be going through many changes, they will still be loved and cared for—only within the new family structure.   **ISBN: 0984541756**

Single Women – Alive and Well!
Dianne Lorang and Ann E. Byrnes

This book is a collection of creative non-fiction stories by and about women who have learned to be strong and happy on their own. These inspirational stories share a common theme: fulfillment comes from within rather than from another person.   **ISBN: 0759601046**

"The best advice I got during my divorce was to take the high road, grin and bare it and never badmouth my former spouse. This has paid off in spades. It kept me from exposing my 'dirty laundry' to the neighborhood, and it kept my children safe from nasty comments and discussions about their parents' divorce. It also made it easier to eventually be friendly with my ex."

RESOURCES

The Divorce Team's Blog
www.DivorceTeam.blogspot.com

David W. Heckenbach, Esq.
Heckenbach/Ammarell, LLP

7400 E. Orchard Rd., Ste 3025N
Greenwood Village, CO 80111
Phone: 303.858.8000
Fax: 303.858.8001
www.FamilyLawColorado.com

Kim Langelaar
Certified Divorce Financial Analyst™
& Mediator

P.O. BOX 3725
Parker, Co 80134
Phone: 303.805.7392
Fax: 720.851.8803
Kim@ColoradoDivorceSolutions.com
www.ColoradoDivorceSolutions.com

Kurt Groesser, Realtor ®, MBA

Phone: 303.481.4222
Kurtgroesser@KW.com
www.GranthamHomeTeam.com

Jan Parsons
Senior Mortgage Banker

4600 S. Ulster, Ste. 300
Denver, CO 80237
Phone: 720.308.1320
Fax: 303.741.2150
JParsons@FirsTierBank.com
www.FirsTierBank.com

Kristine Turner, Ph.D.

558 Castle Pines Pkwy., Unit B4, #364
Castle Rock, CO 80108
Phone: 303.706.9424
Fax: 303.814.3180
Kristine@NewBeginningsCoParenting.com
www.NewBeginningsCoParenting.com
www.DivorceAdviceforChildren.com
www.CastleRockRadio.com

ORDER FORM

The Guide to a
Smart Divorce

$14.95 + 3.50 (S&H)

online at: www.DivorceAdvice360.com

by phone: 303.794.8888

by fax: 720.863.2013

by mail:
send check payable to:
Thornton Publishing, Inc.
17011 Lincoln Ave. #408
Parker, CO 80134

If it is temporarily sold out at your favorite bookstore,
have them order more of ISBN: 0-9846342-0-7

Name: _____

Address: _____

_____

Phone: _____

E-mail: _____

Credit Card #: _____

Card Type: _____   Expiration Date: ____/ ____

Security Code: _____